Cryptocurrency:

5 Expert Secrets for Beginners: Investing into Bitcoin, Ethereum and Litecoin

Anthony Tu

© **Copyright 2017 - All rights reserved.**

The contents of this book may not be reproduced, duplicated or transmitted without direct written permission from the author.

Under no circumstances will any legal responsibility or blame be held against the publisher for any reparation, damages, or monetary loss due to the information herein, either directly or indirectly.

Legal Notice:

This book is copyright protected. This is only for personal use. You cannot amend, distribute, sell, use, quote or paraphrase any part or the content within this book without the consent of the author.

Disclaimer Notice:

Please note the information contained within this document is for educational and entertainment purposes only. Every attempt has been made to provide accurate, up to date and reliable complete information. No warranties of any kind are expressed or implied. Readers acknowledge that the author is not engaging in the rendering of legal, financial, medical or professional advice. The content of this book has been derived from various sources. Please consult a licensed professional before attempting any techniques outlined in this book.

By reading this document, the reader agrees that under no circumstances are is the author responsible for any losses, direct or indirect, which are incurred as a result of the use of information contained within this document, including, but not limited to, —errors, omissions, or inaccuracies

For more information, go to www.wonpublications.com

Table of Content

About the Author 1

Introduction 2

Chapter 1: Basics of Cryptocurrency 4
   Rise of Cryptocurrency 5
   Cryptocurrency as Money 7

Chapter 2: Important Terminology 8
   Bloackchain 8
   Bitcoin 10
   Mining 11
   Ethereum 12
   Litecoin 12

Chapter 3: Benefits and Risks of Investing 14
   Benefits 14
   Risks 16

Chapter 4: Expert Secrets 21
   Safeguard against Threats 21
   Invest in Cryptocurrencies with Longevity 23
   Focus on Platform, not just Features 24
   Don't make an Emotional Decision 25
   Don't go all in 27

Conclusion 29

Actions to Take 30

About the Author

Anthony Tu is a financial investor, entrepreneur and philanthropist. Born in Australia from Vietnamese parents, he completed his bachelor of commerce at Curtin University of Technology in Australia, which he focused on Economics and Finance. Over the last 10 years he's been investing in different equities, such as stocks, bonds, and most notably cryptocurrencies.

His passion is to inspire and empowering individuals with his vast wealth of knowledge within the financial sector. From travelling the world, going to seminars, and meeting individuals such as Tony Robbins, he believes empowering individuals to take charge of their finances is crucial in order to become free and live a happy life.

In recent years, his focus has switched towards cryptocurrency investment as seen in his work which he believes offers the best return on investment for the average investor. His goal is to educate individuals about cryptocurrency technologies, and how to invest and make money on various cryptocurrencies.

Outside of work, Anthony can be seen in local community events. He states; "When I'm free, I love to give back to the community. If we have the chance to help others, then help others. We are luckier than most people in this world."

Introduction

I want to thank you for choosing this book, '*Cryptocurrency: 5 Expert Secrets for Beginners: Investing into Bitcoin, Ethereum and Litecoin - Bitcoin, Blockchain, Ethereum, Cryptocurrency, and Litecoin.*' I know you'll find this book valuable on your journey to learning about cryptocurrencies. If you really find this book helpful, please leave an honest review on Amazon.

Cryptocurrencies are a craze right now, and they present an attractive investment opportunity for anyone with some extra cash. Cryptocurrencies are gaining more and more legitimacy as they are legalized, and regulatory authorities are stepping in to maintain order.

Cryptocurrencies are the new means of exchange that only function in the digital world. It's a whole new monetary system that is entirely different from the one we are used it. It is based on cryptography, digital signatures and addresses to conduct transactions. These transactions help keep the users anonymous, which protects their privacy from the eyes of the state. That doesn't mean these cryptocurrencies are always used for illegal dealings – there is a central ledger to most of these currencies, which helps make transactions traceable without giving information on the users.

2009 was the year when cryptocurrencies truly took off. It was all because of Satoshi Nakamoto – the founder of the famous cryptocurrency known as Bitcoin. He came up with a decentralized system where peer-to-peer networking was used to conduct transactions instead of a central figure directing everything.

Bitcoin is the most famous cryptocurrency right now, but thanks to its technology, thousands of other similar currencies have also cropped up. These cryptocurrencies are known as altcoins. A lot of them are just poor copies of Bitcoin, but some have made modifications and updates to make the technology even better. This includes Litecoin, Ethereum, Ripple and Dogecoin.

When it comes to investing in these cryptocurrencies, many people have a lot of doubts and questions. They aren't sure about the risks involved, and are confused by the rumors they have heard. The aim of this book is to solve this problem.

In this book, we will first familiarize you with the concepts of cryptocurrency, explain the various benefits and risks that come with it, and tell you five secrets you need to follow while investing. Let's get started!

Chapter One: Basics of Cryptocurrency

Cryptocurrency is the name given to any digital currency that is deemed secure because of cryptography — or a particular kind of encryption method that's perfect for the whole blockchain process. What's amazing about cryptocurrencies is that no central authorities govern them. They are organic and are a perfect system on their own. The government or anyone not involved in Blockchain cannot manipulate them in any way—keeping your funds always in check.

One thing about cryptocurrency transactions is that they might be used for illicit activities — such as tax evasion or even money laundering. But the main argument towards cryptocurrencies is the ability for parties to easily send and accept funds from each other, even in cryptocurrency form, and only with minimal transaction fees. There are also many other uses for cryptocurrency, including crowdfunding and online voting. After all, people find it easier to spend online currencies instead of real ones— they don't cause too much hassle either.

Cryptocurrency is money created by the use of encryption techniques of advanced computer programming. These same techniques are used to carry out and verify the transfer of funds. Cryptocurrencies are independent of central banks and are decentralized. This means that parties can send and receive funds directly towards each other without a middle man.

In 2009, Bitcoin became the first practicable cryptocurrency, proving that a decentralized currency could exist. This is ironic; given that Bitcoin inventor Satoshi Nakamoto never set out to create a new form of money. He wanted to solve the problem of centralized digital cash and created a peer-to-peer digital cash system. He ended up developing Bitcoin, an entirely unregulated form of currency, which relied upon extensive mathematical computations to validate authenticity. It was with the birth of Bitcoin that cryptocurrency became a reality.

The implications of cryptocurrency are so great that some central banks have attempted to involve themselves in the technology. However, the currency they produce is not officially considered cryptocurrency as they can only develop centralized money. The proponents of cryptocurrency are very keen on keeping the "true" digital currency decentralized.

Rise of Cryptocurrency

Cryptocurrency, such as Bitcoin, Ethereum, Litecoin and others, have had a lot of publicity. As the levels of financial/digital literacy of the general population have increased, cryptocurrency acceptance has also made leaps in purchasing power. In 2010, a Bitcoin investor, known as Laslo, claimed to have purchased two pizzas for roughly 10,000 Bitcoins. It was considered the first instance where a cryptocurrency was used to make a purchase. At the time, Bitcoins were virtually worthless. As of October 2017, Bitcoin is valued higher than gold, with one-coin worth more than $5000.

At first, most were very skeptical of Bitcoin and its technology, seeing it as a form of counterfeit or a device of criminals. This was particularly so when it was publicized as the means of trade on the 'Silk Road,' a part of the dark internet where all sorts of unsavory behavior was rampant.

However, there is now an increasing involvement of legitimate business and government with cryptocurrency. New applications and even ATM's are incorporated to allow cryptocurrency transactions to occur. As a consequence, the market capitalization of all cryptocurrencies is more than $150,000,000,000!

By Mid 2017, we have seen a rise in cryptocurrencies, revealing more than 1000 cryptocurrencies. Most people have heard of Bitcoin, especially since recent ransomware attacks have demanded payment in Bitcoins. The benefit to criminals of this is that any such payment by a victim would be untraceable.

If the website for coinmarketcap is checked, it will be seen that there is a small graph beside the type of cryptocurrency, each showing the movement of the currency in the last week, as well as the percentage change in the last 24 hours. It will be seen that there is a significant disparity in the values of the various cryptocurrencies with one Bitcoin being worth more than $5000 and a total market capitalization of more than $80,000,000,000. Another cryptocurrency called Bytecoin was worth less than one cent although the total capitalization of Bytecoins was more than $200,000,000. Some cryptocurrencies have small capitalizations. An example is MikeTheMug cryptocurrency with a capitalization of less than $1000! We will have more to say about the quality and worth of cryptocurrencies later.

Cryptocurrency as Money

The people involved in cryptocurrency call the currencies we use, in everyday life, 'fiat.' Despite the word 'currency' in the word cryptocurrency, there are greater similarities between cryptocurrencies and stocks than cryptocurrencies and fiat currencies. A purchase of some cryptocurrency is a purchase of a technology stock, an entry in a digital ledger called a blockchain, and a part of the digital network for that cryptocurrency.

Cryptocurrency is a means of exchange that uses cryptography so that transactions are secure and to exercise control over the manufacture of further units of the currency. Cryptocurrencies are a type of what is called alternative currencies.

Due to their frequent and great fluctuations in value, one of the two fundamentals of money, namely "a store of value" is lacking. Some digital currencies exhibit the behavior of countries having significant inflation in that value is not retained.

Chapter Two: Important Terminology

Blockchain

Blockchain is what encompasses all transactions of cryptocurrencies, most prominently Bitcoin. The blockchain is a public record that solely exists in the digital world— which means you wouldn't get any physical coins of any sort. If you need to buy something online, and you're allowed to pay cryptocurrencies for it, then you will be able to get that item even without real cash— as long as you have enough cryptocurrency.

One of the main things about Blockchain is that it allows you to have this sense of ownership over something, even if you do not have it in your hands, and you also have the capacity to transfer ownership to someone else when you get the proper Blockchain record done. You also have to realize that once a transaction is done, then it is there forever. What happens in the Blockchain stays in the Blockchain— and that's how it will always be.

You can get cryptocurrencies either by accepting, trading or mining for them. When it comes to mining, you can think of it as how mining is done in real life— or the way of looking for what it is you need. In this case, the computer will be the one doing the mining and will be working through complex situations to help you find what you are looking for.

Miners will then make use of a collection of transactions by organizing them in one block alone. Now, with the help of these blocks— and information— the chain (Blockchain) gets to be created, which means that there will no longer be any kind of inconsistencies. There won't be any bad or bouncing checks or anything that would make transactions full of hassle. Self-Regulation is also easily done, as blockchain systems make regular inspections to make way for secure transactions because several confirmations are done before a transaction is made— safer than your usual bank or remittance transactions.

What you have to understand about Blockchain is that one computer alone does not just handle transactions— there is no "central" or "main" bank here. They are managed by distributed nodes or pathways that are then in charge of having copies of everything that happens in the blockchain, together with the users who have created those records, so that copies will be synchronized and will easily be understood by the system— making transactions seamless and easy.

So, for example, your Bitcoins are all lined up in one row, so even if they are not currently in use, the Blockchain can make something out of them, always keeping them in check, and always keeping you and other users as top priority. Transactions are also not done on standard systems— specialized hardware is used for them.

Many people believe that in the future, more people would be making use of the Blockchain system, in particular with the emergence of many companies online, mostly those that employ amazing technology. With the help of a great transaction ledger, such as blockchain, it might be used by international communications systems— to make sure that transactions become safer and easier to do.

Bitcoin

One of the first digital currencies around was created back in 2009. The infamous Satoshi Nakamoto, who, even today is suspected of being perhaps more than one person, created Bitcoin. It was created as a means to provide a new way of making online payments and transactions, which is not operated by the government and is decentralized— you will learn more about it in the succeeding chapter of this book! As of October 2017, the total of Bitcoins has amounted to over 16.6 million, which means that it would be a whopping $83.4 billion in market value.

What you can keep in mind now is that you will never be able to hold Bitcoins physically and that they are operated by private keys— or strings of letters and numbers that are linked by an encrypted algorithm. For this, you would be using a public key— like one of those bank account numbers, which would then act as the address of your transaction. There are also two ways of writing Bitcoin. Bitcoin, with a capitalized B, talks about the concept or identity of cryptocurrencies, while Bitcoin, with a small letter b, is about the amount of currency being used. It could also be abbreviated to BTC (Bitcoin Transaction). Sometimes, the letters XBT are also used.

A lot of people say that Bitcoin stands out from the rest because of its extremely safe online ledger that cannot be accessed by hackers, making you confident that no one will be able to copy your data because only private keys are used for this.

Mining

This is the primary process of adding and verifying transactions so they can be placed in the blockchain, otherwise known as a public ledger so that new Bitcoins can also be released. Anyone, as long as the person has reliable internet access, could try mining for Bitcoins.

Back in the day, regular desktop CPUs were used for mining, but these days, Graphic Processing Units (GPUs) are mostly used, together with Application Specific Integrated Circuit (ASIC), hardware that's designed specifically for the process of mining Bitcoins.

What happens during a mining session is that recent transactions are compiled so that a puzzle can potentially be solved in the right manner, and once that puzzle is solved, then Bitcoins can be released. It's like a contest where the first person that guesses right will then win Bitcoins, as a prize, also known as block rewards. The difficulty of puzzles depends on the kind of effort that's introduced in the network and is adjusted per week— to make sure that no one will cheat, and block rewards will be given only to those who deserve them. Block Rewards also stand for each block that has been mined, which could then be halved every four years— or for every 210,000 blocks. These will then be used for transaction fees, so you will not have to pay extra.

Ethereum

One of the newest parts of the blockchain is Ethereum, which has gained large popularity in 2017, becoming the second most traded cryptocurrency. Ethereum is a software platform that's decentralized which was released in 2015. It is something that enables distributed applications and smart contacts to be built without control, downtime, or any form of fraud. So more than just being a part of blockchain, Ethereum also acts as a programming language that completely runs on the blockchain, and is responsible for helping developers improve and publish more blockchain mechanisms— so that the future of blockchain will certainly be brighter.

What you have to understand about applications that run on this platform is that they are mostly used by people who are trying to develop new apps. So, currencies can be exchanged, and work can easily be monetized, decentralized, and be secure so that trying to access the system won't be too hard for those who need and are allowed to access it.

Litecoin

With a market cap of over $ 3.5 Billion as of October 2017, Litecoin deems itself to be the second best CryptoCurrency program out there - second to Bitcoin, much like the silver to gold. Litecoin transactions happen in a fast and secure manner — perfect for those who hate waiting a little too long just to send or receive money. Specialized and safe computer hardware is also used to make this happen.

A former Google employee by the name of Charlie Lee released Litecoin on Github in 2011. The main difference between Bitcoin and Litecoin is the time taken to process a block. Litecoin reduces the time taken to 2.5 minutes, while Bitcoin still takes 10 minutes. The Litecoin network has also been programmed to produce four times as many currency units as Bitcoin, making Litecoin four times faster.

If you're finding this book helpful, please leave an honest review on Amazon. Thank you.

Chapter Three: Benefits and Risks of Investing

Benefits

Financial Self-Determinism and Control

The cryptocurrency networks are one of a kind because they are a digital store of value where people can securely save cryptocurrency units and enter into transactions without the need to rely on any third party regulatory body. After you have acquired and safely secured your cryptocurrency units, it is almost impossible for other people (thieves, hackers, banks or even the government) to take them away from you. The government cannot authorize the freezing of your cryptocurrency account nor stop you from entering into any transactions within the cryptocurrency network.

Lower Cost of Transactions

While frozen accounts may be problematic, you also need to be aware of the cost of getting a transaction ready for use. On top of the unexpected risks of frozen accounts and massive chargebacks when you use payment processors, you will also be exposed to well-known high transaction charges for the services of these payment processors. This can considerably reduce the income of your business.

The transaction charges of PayPal, Google Checkout and Amazon Checkout all begin at 2.9 percent plus $ 0.30 for each transaction. You can enjoy a lower rate of 1.9 percent only if your total transactions for the month amount to more than $30,000. Because of this, these exorbitant fees may burden a business with a low-profit margin. The same goes for businesses that require a lot of smaller transactions or those whose products are sold at a nominal price.

In contrast to current day transactions, cryptocurrencies are known for their low fees, a major reason why banks are looking to adopt them. The fees vary according to which cryptocurrency is being traded. Bitcoin is known for their high fees relative to other cryptocurrencies, however, Ethereum and Litecoin can have fees less than 1%. This is important because even though 1-2% may not seem like a lot, when compounded interest is taken place over years, this could equate to thousands, and even millions on large scale trading.

It Works Around the World

The cryptocurrency network is considered to be an intrinsically wide-reaching and global network. One of the biggest arguments for cryptocurrencies is the fast and low-cost transaction speeds across the world. You will not have to pass through artificial barriers to make payments to vendors who are based in other countries or regions. In fact, it is not entirely possible to validate where a particular cryptocurrency transaction originated. An online vendor who accepts cryptocurrency units as a mode of payment can instantly gain access to a global market while facing the risk of non-payment from customers who reside outside his own country and who are not bound by the legal system of his government. For example, this will allow individuals from the United States to send money to people in Australia in less than 10 minutes, making this much more convenient than third party transactions which are costly.

You should be aware of whether the cryptocurrency in your area is valid and viable for use. The legal status of the cryptocurrency will vary based on the country you get your transaction in.

Risks

Volatility of Cryptocurrency Prices

When someone asks you what the value of the cryptocurrency units that you own is, how can you readily answer the question? The fundamental value of any particular currency is a function of the consumer demand for that currency and the consumers' capability to use the currency to trade it for valuable goods and services. Because a lot of conventional currencies are no longer linked to the worth of an underlying product or commodity such as gold and other precious metals, a cryptocurrency unit will only be valuable when some people or consumers want to own them and use them for trade.

Currently, there are plenty of public exchanges that have been set up to allow consumers to buy and sell cryptocurrency units in exchange for dollars or other common currencies. This aids in establishing a fundamental relative value for cryptocurrencies, which then allow vendors to convert their cryptocurrency holdings into other common currencies on a more regular basis. This minimizes the vendors' risk exposure to the price volatility of cryptocurrencies.

Even though during the recent years, the price of cryptocurrencies has significantly fluctuated, there now exist methods that vendors can use to quote cryptocurrency prices relative to their equivalent value in dollar or other common currency. This also allows them to convert the cryptocurrencies they have collected into another currency immediately.

This comparatively small market limitation together with the absence of a regulatory body may expose the prices of cryptocurrencies to become manipulated by the market players. It's like what you would expect out of penny stocks and other items that are not as commonplace; it only takes one or two transactions for the values of certain items to be jacked up and artificially influenced.

Several important speculations are being made in various online forums on who may be behind the price manipulation of cryptocurrencies and to what extent. It is quite common to hear cryptocurrency speculators refer to "The Manipulator" when they discuss significant market movements.

"The Manipulator" refers to an unidentified individual or group of people that are assumed to be controlling the cryptocurrency prices through their vast wealth. But it is not clear as to who these people are.

One thing is for certain that the relatively anonymous nature of the cryptocurrency is a huge part of what allows people to adjust the values of cryptocurrencies as they see fit. This makes for an added risk to the cryptocurrency. Of course, whoever is regulating it could always stop doing so and focus on some other kind of investment in the future, but it can be next to impossible to figure out what's going to happen.

Risk of Loss

When you own cryptocurrency units, it is quite apparent that you have the responsibility to ensure that your digital wallet is secured from any potential hazards of loss and theft. This task or responsibility can be quite taxing, especially if you own a substantial number of cryptocurrencies because you will have to use certain tools such as protected encryption, password management and information backup to make sure that your risks are maintained at a low-level.

Several high-profile incidents have already been reported where people made errors and mistakes in handling their cryptocurrency accounts that ultimately led to them losing a large amount of their cryptocurrencies. Since there is no central authority you can approach to seek help or assistance, you may have to completely write off your losses because they may already be unrecoverable.

The risks associated with cryptocurrencies are critical and have to be identified. It should not be a surprise that a virtual currency that is relatively new is in danger of being hacked into.

You should be cautious when seeing how this currency is run before you make any trades with it.

Regulatory Ambiguity

The legal category of cryptocurrencies remains uncertain. Some people consider it as a commodity like gold and silver while other treat it as a viable currency. Still, there are others who look at them as a financial product or something that is legally equal to the gold in World of Warcraft. It is yet to be known if they will someday require licenses and financial rules and regulations for it to become a truly viable currency.

Mt.Gox, which was considered as the biggest Bitcoin exchange market, has reported that they have experienced some difficulties in wiring funds. This is because of certain money laundering investigations done by the government or regulatory agencies.

But cryptocurrencies are intrinsically difficult to regulate because no central authority oversees all transactions. Because of this, it is highly probable that cryptocurrencies can become the primary medium option for people who are into illicit activities such as money laundering and tax evasion.

What makes the cryptocurrency market such a concern is that the protected nature of the currency makes it popular among those who engage in illegal or questionable activities.

But if we stop and think about it, any paper currency such as the US dollar can also have the same risks as described above. It is also possible to complete illegal transactions anonymously using dollar bills because it is possible to exchange it without any auditable paper trails. But the complexity of the cryptocurrency network technology may instigate regulators to see it as a hazard to the rules of law.

Chapter Four: Expert Secrets

It is possible to compare the growth in cryptocurrency technology to the internet boom in the late 1990s. However, some think it could be more. During 2016, the market capitalization of the total cryptocurrency increased by more than 50% in about six months. During the first half of 2017, most cryptocurrencies grew more than 1000%! This seemed unreal, however since its peak in June, the market has found more stability. The statistics on the growth of the top 100 cryptocurrencies are mouth-watering for an investor.

Often there are more to these cryptocurrency projects than the transfer of digital currency, some of them add to or supplant existing processes with much better results. In the years to come, there will be a huge number of conventional and outmoded models, which will be replaced by cryptocurrency-based methods. Investors who are wise will try and decide those cryptocurrency projects that satisfy a real need, and those which are nothing more than fads. If you want to invest in cryptocurrencies, here are five expert secrets that will help you out:

Safeguard against Threats

Anything in the world of technology can be hacked into if plenty of effort is made and cryptocurrencies are no exception to this. One such example comes from how hackers stole about $ 1.2 million in Bitcoins from Inputs.io recently. This came as a result of hacking software designed to find information on the ownership status of Bitcoins. This allowed the hackers to steal the money. Another incident was the infamous Mt Gox hack which saw 850,000 bitcoins stolen from accounts, a value worth $460,000,000 at the time or $4.25 Billion today!

What makes this worse is that cryptocurrencies are like cash in that they will be gone without any way to easily replace them if they are stolen. What makes this even worse is that it will be hard for anyone to recoup losses if items are stolen. This creates a strong need to ensure that added protection is used when you are investing.

To protect yourself from any potential online threats, please consider protecting yourself with the following considerations:

- Consider using an online 'soft' wallet. Online wallets by name, are wallets created by 3rd parties that are based online. They are protected through various codes and set keys that is given to the individual. You can think of them as a cloud storage, much like iCloud, google drive, most soft wallets are easy to sign use, and there are plenty. Some include, Exodus and Jaxx.
- Transfer any cryptocurrencies that are earned to an offline hardware device. Offline hardware wallets are made to protect individuals from digital hackers. If you are very paranoid about the digital world, I would highly recommend a hardware wallet. Keep in mind that these hard wallets are physical, meaning that if it is lost, it is

impossible to recover them. So keep them safe. They are much like USB sticks which contain all your cryptocurrencies on a hardware device. One of the most popular hardware wallet is the Ledger Nano S. For more information, follow the link below, https://www.ledgerwallet.com/r/737d

- Consider getting an encrypted cloud storage service to work on your account.

If you aren't comfortable about this, then you can always exchange your cryptocurrencies for cash. You can do this online through any exchange or through different cryptocurrency ATMs depending on where you live and what is available for when you take care of the transaction.

Invest in Cryptocurrencies with Longevity

There are numerous rules you should obey when investing, with some of greater importance than others. The first is the rule of longevity. In highly volatile markets, investing long term allows you to hedge against short term fluctuations. This allows you as an investor to reduce risks. Within the cryptocurrency market, it is very volatile, and depending on the type of investor you are, you can profit on this, however, you can also lose a lot. It is highly recommended to look at the long term prospects. When selecting a long-term investment, you must choose projects that have this; you must examine not only the product but also those who produced it. You must understand what it is you're investing in and ask: is this service going to be needed or utilized in the years ahead? Is there any competition that will easily outdo this project? Do the developers show commitment? Until you understand what you are truly investing in, there is a lot of risk involved. The multi billionaire Warren Buffet once said

"Never invest in a business you cannot understand."

These are the three things you need to focus on to determine if a project is worth considering or not:

- A current or developing demand for it – For a project to be valuable there has to be a market value. This is determined by the demand of the project.
- No serious competition – Any serious competition will reduce the potential growth of the project.
- Developers with commitment – When investing in anything, whether companies, cryptocurrencies, or stocks, it's important to know who is in charge of operations. Strong leaders will see the company progress faster. A good example is Elon Musk of Tesla and SpaceX, as well as Steve Jobs of Apple. Within cryptocurrency, a good example is Vitalik Buterin, the founder of Ethereum.

Focus on Platform, not just Features

This is very important, as a lot of the current cryptocurrency projects are merely full of features, but don't offer a platform of significance. You may well ask what on Earth is meant by a platform. By platform, we mean a cryptocurrency that has a number of different services. In other words, it does or facilitates something apart from being electronic money. Some cryptocurrencies are geared to a particular market such as betting or legal marijuana.

Today there are only 20 to 30 viable cryptocurrency projects, meaning the remaining hundreds are of little use as investments with long-term prospects. cryptocurrencies such as Bitcoin or Ethereum, with tremendous momentum and support, are platforms.

In assessing a cryptocurrency, compare it to the large cryptocurrency platforms like Bitcoin or Ethereum. Ask yourself does the project compare favorably? Is the project well established and does it have a reputation? If it does not, then probably it is not a good long-term investment.

The long term prices of cryptocurrencies are determined by the potential of the projects. So small scale projects have less potential, thus will less likely increase in value over time.

Understand Fees

In the previous chapter we run through the importance of fees. It cannot be emphasized enough how important it is to find exchanges with low fees. Every percentage does matter, and if you're looking to invest regularly, this should be the number one advice you should take. The difference between a 1% and 3% in fees can equate to a 50% reducing in return on investment extended periods of time. This is due to the nature of *compounding interest*. Some exchanges are made easy for your convenience. They make it easy for new users to understand and use, but this comes at a cost. One popular exchange is Coinbase. Though Coinbase is very simple to use, they have one of the highest fees at around 3.99%. If you must get your cryptocurrency now, it is made for convenience. However, it is not recommended as there are many exchanges with less than 1% fees. Don't be afraid to look around for cheaper exchanges and educate yourself on how to use them. Keep in mind some exchanges lower the prices of the cryptocurrency but it cost more after fees are implemented. For example,

Coinbase: BTC/USD: $3500 + Fees: 3.99% = $3639.65

Other exchanges: BTC/USD: $3550 + Fees: 0.99% = $3585.145

As you can see on the example, other exchanges have a market price of $3550 on the BTC/USD exchange, a $50 higher valuation than Coinbase. Keep in mind that those fees play a huge role. With fees implemented, Coinbase comes out at just over $50 higher! One thing you should also consider is the opportunity cost involved. That difference of $50 can be reinvested thus the potential gains from reinvestment is also lost when investing in Coinbase.

Don't make an Emotional Decision

If you want to invest, you should never make emotional decisions, especially in the cryptocurrency market. Firstly, the most common problem people have when investing is the Fear Of Missing Out (FOMO). It is this fear that drives people to make irrational decisions. It drives them to invest more than they can afford, make poor decisions, and overthink. You can see this also as human greed. When the market is blowing up and increasing at 10% per day, people want to get in, it's natural. But understand that the market always punishes greed and rewards the patient. In a highly volatile market such as cryptocurrencies, FOMO is what allows people to lose money. They get in when there is hype, and they run away and panic sell when things are going down. You should remember what your outcome is, your strategy and focus on the long term.

You should only invest a percentage of your money after doing a lot of research. This percentage is of course very subjective and depends on a number of factors. Although cryptocurrency has a lot of stories where people who only invested a little made fortunes, its volatility means that to get the best results you have to manage your investments. Do not invest more than you can afford to lose, particularly if the whole world of investment is new to you. It is so easy to underestimate the risks posed by this volatility. Experiment with a small sum like $20 until you know what you're doing.

Here is a suggestion:

If you are less than 30 years old, then no more than 30% cryptocurrency, with a good 50% in safe investments (don't hesitate to seek good advice about what is safe)

If you're in the age range 30 – 40 years old, then no more than 20% cryptocurrency and 60% in Traditional Investments

If you're older than 40 years old, then retirement should be a serious consideration, and you should not have more than 10% cryptocurrency, and you should have at least 70% in Traditional Investments

This is subject to many things like the job you have, the amount of experience you have in investing, your home situation, when you propose to retire, etc.

Even inside your cryptocurrency portfolio, you should have different coins; there are plenty to choose from. This process is called 'spreading your risk.' Never forget the old saying about not putting all your eggs in only one basket.

Conclusion

If you are going to invest in cryptocurrencies, the first thing to focus on is research. You have to make judgments for yourself instead of relying on all the information that you have been given. It is after all your money – make sure that you're investing in something worthwhile. So, always look into the history, future and trade practices of the cryptocurrency before making any decisions.

You should also remember that you don't need to invest in only the famous cryptocurrencies. Everybody knows about Bitcoin, and they all want to get in on it. This means that the returns on Bitcoin might not be as good because even Bitcoin at this point requires a hefty sum of initial investment.

You should focus on the upcoming small players like OmiseGo, Ripple, and Golem. These platforms are highly undervalued considering the potential they have. You can invest in them now at a low price to enjoy the benefits when they blow up.

Thank you for buying this book and if you really found this book helpful, please leave an honest review on Amazon.

All the best!

Actions to Take

Once again, congratulations! Now that you're an expert in the fundamentals of cryptocurrencies. It's time to dive a bit deeper and master the cryptocurrencies. This diverse knowledge will not only benefit you as an individual but enhance your investing abilities. So what makes Bitcoin so valuable? It Primarily has to do with the marketing factor of Bitcoin. It is generally the introductory coin to cryptocurrencies. People hear about Bitcoin before anything else so they buy Bitcoin. As we know, the value of these coins are determined by the buyers.

If you are interested in learning taking your knowledge to the next level, check out my other book, *'Mastering Bitcoin: The Ultimate guide for Beginners to Understanding Bitcoin Technology, Bitcoin Investing, Bitcoin Mining and Other Cryptocurrencies.'*

In this Ultimate guide, we will first familiarize you with everything from the history of Bitcoin, Bitcoin mining, Bitcoin Technology and the benefits and risks involved with investing in Bitcoin. As a BONUS, you will find out how cryptocurrencies were formed from Bitcoin.
Master Bitcoin today!
You can find this on the Kindle store;
ASIN: B076DF24SD

Ethereum is the leading platform developer of ICO's (Initial Coin Offering). This means that most coins that are newly released are operated on the Ethereum network, approximately 75% of total coins released. This uncapped potential has seen Ethereum has seen an explosion in value in the course of 2017, from $8 in January to $300 in October.

If you want to know more about the leading cryptocurrency platform developer, check out my other book, *'Mastering Ethereum: The Ultimate guide for Beginners to Understanding Ethereum Technology, Ethereum Investing, Ethereum Mining and Other Cryptocurrencies.'*

Master the second largest cryptocurrency today!
You can find this on the Kindle store;
ASIN: B076W27PT6

Made in the USA
Lexington, KY
12 November 2017